RAINDROP STORIES

by Preston R. Bassett
with Margaret Farrington Bartlett

illustrated by Jim Arnosky

FOUR WINDS PRESS   NEW YORK

Library of Congress Cataloging in Publication Data

Bassett, Preston R
  Raindrop stories.

  Summary: Follows Johnny Raindrop through a gentle spring shower, a hailstorm, a summer thunderstorm, an autumn rain, and an ice storm.
  1. Rain and rainfall—Juvenile literature. 2. Storms—Juvenile literature. [1. Rain and rainfall. 2. Precipitation (Meteorology)] I. Bartlett, Margaret Farrington, joint author. II. Arnosky, Jim. III. Title.
QC924.7.B37   [E]   80-19036
ISBN 0-590-07628-0

PUBLISHED BY FOUR WINDS PRESS
A DIVISION OF SCHOLASTIC INC., NEW YORK, N.Y.
TEXT COPYRIGHT © 1981 BY PRESTON R. BASSETT AND MARGARET FARRINGTON BARTLETT
ILLUSTRATIONS COPYRIGHT © 1981 BY JAMES ARNOSKY
ALL RIGHTS RESERVED
PRINTED IN THE UNITED STATES OF AMERICA
LIBRARY OF CONGRESS CATALOG CARD NUMBER: 80-19036
1 2 3 4 5 85 84 83 82 81

*To my thirteen grandchildren and
my three great-grandchildren—P.R.B.*

An April Shower

It was a lovely spring day. The earth was just waking from its winter sleep. Johnny and his friends were too small to be called raindrops. They were not even big enough to be falling. They floated above the countryside as a small, gray, misty cloud of water vapor, all admiring the sunny fields below.

Johnny was not too small to share his thoughts. "I'm growing rather fast," he said, "and getting heavier. I'm starting to fall!" Johnny looked around and saw that he was not alone. There were many drops keeping him company. They all started to fall past their smaller brothers and sisters who still floated in the cloud.

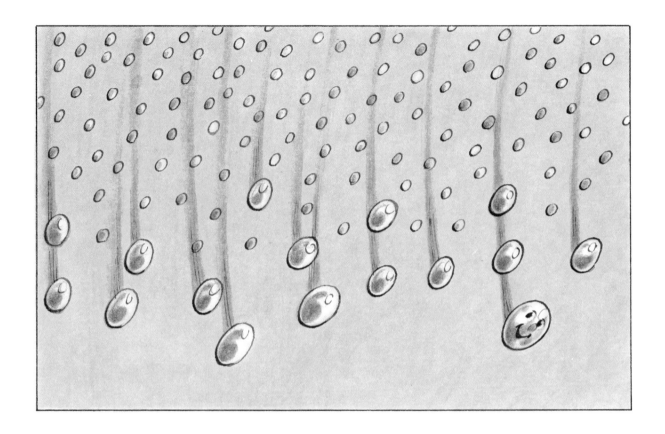

Johnny called out, "Hey, everyone, this is sort of sudden, but I think we're starting on a trip."

He heard the raindrops' faint reply: "We couldn't pick a better time. It's spring — the ground looks thirsty."

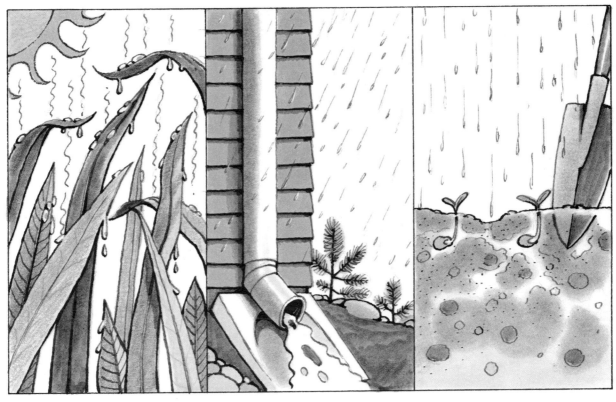

FLY OFFS **RUN OFFS** **SNEAK OFFS**

The raindrops wondered where they would land and what their future would be. Johnny had dropped around a lot and could show off his knowledge. He told his friends, "We've got three main chances: We will either fly off, run off, or sneak off.

"The 'fly offs' land on some surface and wet it. They might land on a rain hat or a fence post. When the sun comes out, the fly offs dry up. They evaporate. They haven't been much use, so they are called back to the sky for another try.

"The 'run offs' are in a big hurry. They are like an overcrowded traffic jam. They fill the gutters and run down the spouts. They rush down the hillsides and empty into rivers and lakes. They are finally in for a long vacation with no hard duties. They are kept in storage.

"The 'sneak offs' get down in the dirt and hide out of sight. They can't be pushed around. They slowly explore trails along slender white tendrils, called roots. Many are sucked up by grass roots. They help grass grow healthy and green."

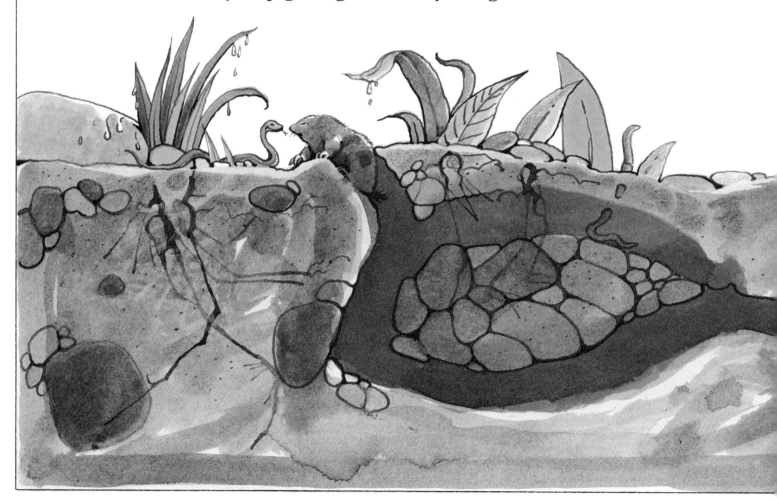

The raindrops had a gentle, easy trip. Some landed on a dry level field — pitter, patter. The earth was ready. The sneak offs went right to work.

"Those raindrops were lifesavers," Johnny said. "When you hear that old saying, 'April showers bring May flowers,' remember the sneak offs. They're a lucky bunch!"

Hailstorm

It was a long summer hot spell. A large cloud hung low over town, and all the air below was humid. The people needed cooling off. If the hot, moisture-laden air could only go up a mile or so, it would be cooled, but the air above the cloud was heavy. Like a blanket, it was holding the cloud, and the air below it, down.

Then intense heat during the noon hour caused a break-through. The cloud found a way to burst through that heavy air blanket. The warm air for miles around became aware of the breakthrough and rushed to join the updraft.

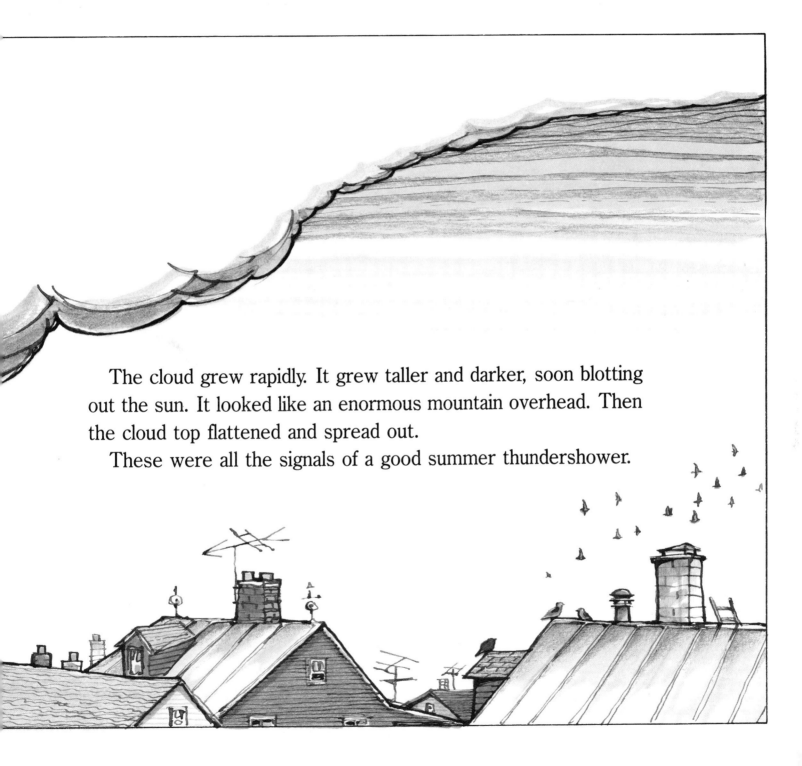

The cloud grew rapidly. It grew taller and darker, soon blotting out the sun. It looked like an enormous mountain overhead. Then the cloud top flattened and spread out.

These were all the signals of a good summer thundershower.

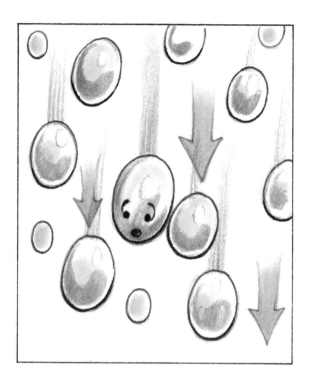

Johnny Raindrop was in the darkest part of this thundershower cloud. The gusty air tossed him around. He thought, "This is going to be an exciting trip." Then he realized that something was wrong. "I fall and fall but I don't get down nearer to the ground. The crazy updraft goes up faster than I fall down." It was a terribly strong wind; the raindrops were being carried up higher and higher. Johnny said, "I bet I'm two miles high. The higher I go, the colder I feel. I wish I could go down."

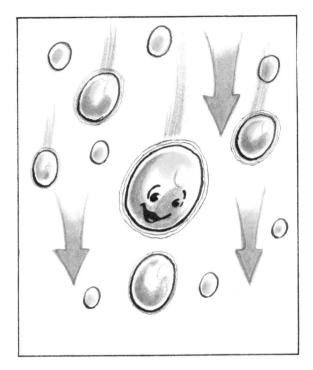 

But that wild updraft wasn't ready to let him go! It blew him higher. Suddenly Johnny called out, "Come on — please let me go! I'm freezing! I'm turning to ice!"

The wind was mischievous. When it let Johnny fall a bit, he bumped into other drops, and was coated with water. Then another cold gust lifted him up and the coating froze like an icy overcoat. After he'd been blown up and down several times, Johnny was much bigger than an ordinary raindrop. He looked like a small onion, or as if he were wearing several layers of icy overcoats.

Finally the wind calmed and let him fall. What a trip! Down, down, down, down, down … Wham! He bounced and rolled on the ground among a lot of other hailstones. Johnny breathed a sigh of relief. All he wanted was to rest in the grass where he could stay quiet until the sun came out to melt him. Then he would fly off, called back to the sky for another adventure.

🌱 *The Secret of Thunder and Lightning*

It was another hot August day. A brisk thunderstorm could cool things off and make everybody more comfortable. The air was carrying a lot of water vapor. This humid air needed an updraft to lift it high enough to squeeze some of the moisture out into a cloud which would grow thicker and darker.

Johnny's adventure started simply enough. As part of that cloud, he and thousands of his little mates were riding in the warm updraft.

They were too small to fall. As the air became cooler, they became larger and larger, until they were good-sized raindrops. But the updraft was strong. It would not let them fall.

The updraft buffeted Johnny around so roughly that he could not keep his shape. He squirmed and wriggled. He became longer and longer. Then he flattened out, all this time struggling to stay in one piece.

Johnny Raindrop could hear the gruff howling of the wind. He shouted, "Oh, please be easy on me; I might break. I do not want to come apart."

"Haw, haw," howled the wind. "This is not an ordinary rainstorm. This is a thunderstorm. I am not through with you!"

So squirming Johnny struggled on. Soon he was too big to stay in one piece. The blustering wind suddenly pulled him into a long pearlike shape.

He struggled to hold together, but his small end broke off. It immediately became a free little droplet, and Johnny again became a manageable size.

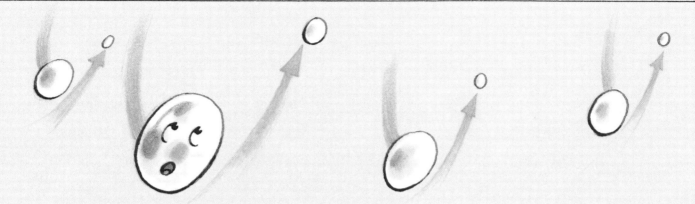

"Well, I'm in control again, but I don't feel quite right. I feel a little tingly. I better see how my broken-off droplet feels. Why, it's way up there. It's light enough to go up with the wind while I'm falling down. We are drifting apart."

Johnny looked around. He saw that all the broken-away pieces were going up with the wind, and all the big drops were falling down. And all the drops, large and small, were tingling with electricity.

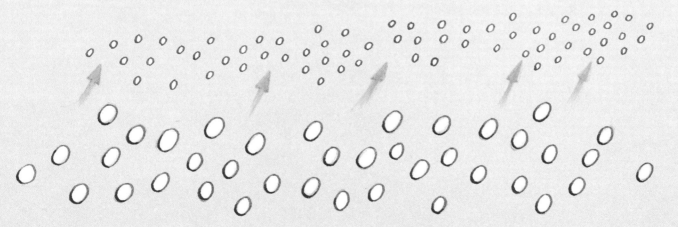

As the separation grew, Johnny's tingling got worse. Suddenly — snap! boom! The cloud exploded. A dazzling electric flash leaped from the upper part of the cloud to the lower part. A clap

of thunder shook every drop. Johnny Raindrop was stunned, but, much to his surprise, his tingling was all gone. He was again his normal self and falling with his crowd of mates, becoming the first heavy burst of rain in the thunderstorm.

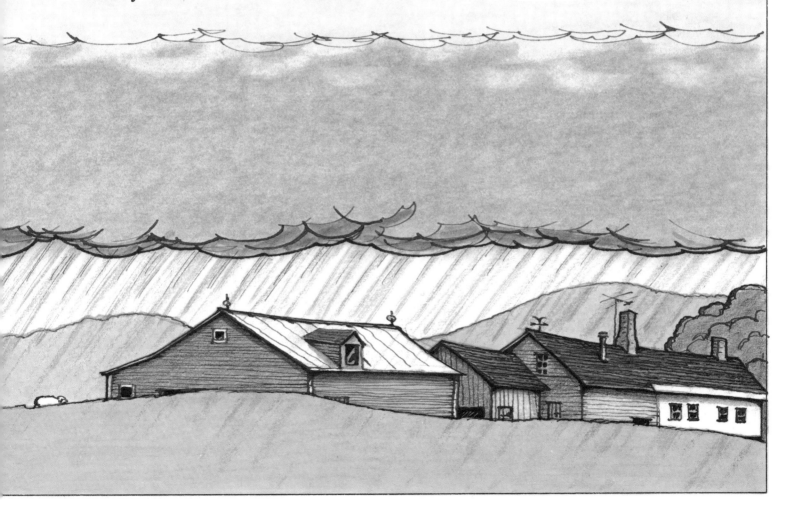

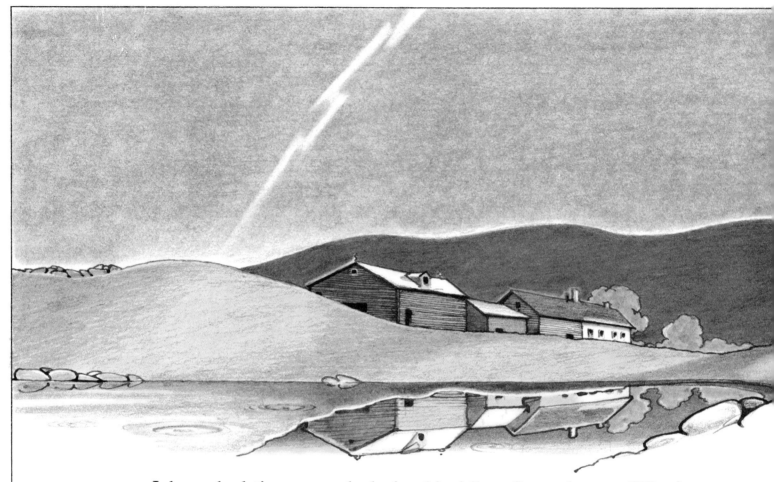

Johnny had time enough during his fall to figure it out: "*That's* the secret of thunder and lightning. The updraft must be strong. It must be rough enough to break apart all of us overgrown raindrops and charge us electrically. That was the tingling I felt, an electric charge. And my broken-off piece had an opposite charge.

"The wind blew us apart, farther and farther, until lightning flashed between us. It knocked the electricity right out of me.

"The flash of lightning was so hot that the air ran out of its way. Then the air rushed back, faster than the speed of sound, making a great boom that echoed through the cloud."

November Rain

It was November. The leaves had all fallen, and the countryside looked bare and forlorn. The sky was gray and overcast from horizon to horizon. The wind came in from over the ocean where it had picked up much moisture as it traveled over miles of restless waves.

Johnny Raindrop was up there, but feeling rather quiet. He wished he could find another exciting adventure like those he had been having.

There were a lot of other raindrops hanging around too, ready to make the same boring trip. "What can we all do?" Johnny asked himself.

He looked down. "If we land in the dirt below we will only make mud. There is nothing growing." He heard the wind whistle, bringing still more moisture from the ocean. The sky got grayer and he started to leave.

Johnny and his mates fell along in a continuous downpour. They were no longer single raindrops. Clinging together, they rushed along in a stream of clear, pure water. After a lively ride they were dumped into a quiet pond of clean water.

Johnny and his friends were run offs. Someday they would find themselves swooshing through fire hoses, swirling into a pitcher

of lemon juice to make lemonade — providing water for the people to use in many different ways. They had landed in the town reservoir.

 *Ice Storm*

It was one of those gray, uncertain winter days. Would it snow or would it rain? Would there be sun? The thermometer stood just at the freezing point.

Johnny Raindrop was falling slowly and aimlessly in the still, quiet air. As he came closer to the ground, he did not feel any wind. But it was cold. A chilly feeling told him he was almost freezing.

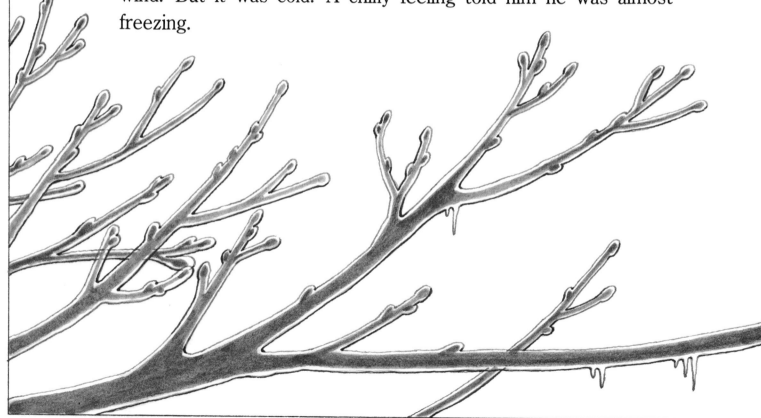

Johnny coasted toward a treetop and noticed that its twigs were coated with ice. "How strange," he thought. "They're all frozen, and yet here I am still a drop of water. My goodness! I'm getting too close. Help!"

Johnny brushed against the twig. "Oh, excuse me, please let me go." It was too late. The ice grabbed him and spread him thin like a coating. He froze immediately, becoming part of a crystal twig.

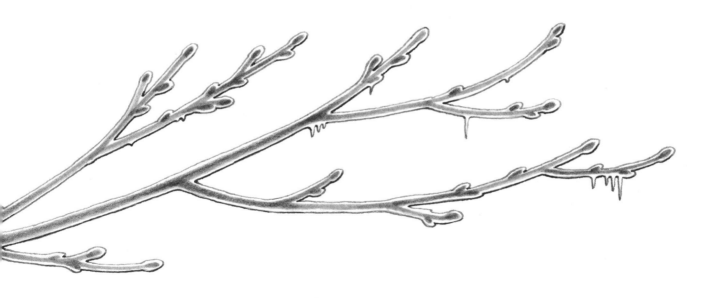

"Stay with us," the tree branches seemed to murmur. "We look so beautiful when the sun shines." So Johnny rested. Soon the sun came out. It quickly found the ice-coated tree and made it sparkle. What a sight!

Many children stopped at the tree on their way home from school. Its sparkling branches made them curious. They ran their mittened hands along the icy twigs. The top branches glistened like diamonds.

From his ice-covered branch, Johnny remembered: "I've often said we raindrops must either fly off, run off, or sneak off. But now we have a new trick — we can show off. What a lovely way to end the year!"

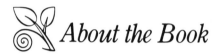 *About the Book*

These stories about raindrops were told by Preston R. Bassett to his four children when they were young. At the time Mr. Bassett was chief engineer, soon to be president, of the Sperry Gyroscope Company, which he joined as a researcher in 1915. One of his studies, which resulted in the patent for high power searchlights, included a thorough investigation of the weather and the functions of raindrops.

Margaret Farrington Bartlett, then science teacher at the Dalton School and later editor for the *Science Is What and Why* series, heard the stories. An author distinguished for such books as *Down the Mountain, Rock All Around*, and *Who Will Answer the Owl?*, she felt they had an irresistible imaginative appeal, but she wondered about their educational value.

When it turned out that each of Mr. Bassett's children went on to pursue successful careers in scientific fields, she became convinced that the stories should be written down and published for others to share.

Mr. Bassett lives in Ridgefield, Connecticut, and Margaret Farrington Bartlett lives in Rutland, Vermont. They corresponded for over a year, transposing these oral stories into suitable prose and deciding upon the ones that appear here.

For *Raindrop Stories*, Jim Arnosky pictured the town and fields that surround his home in South Ryegate, Vermont. There the artist lives with his wife and daughters on a farm called "Ramtails," overlooking the Wells River Valley Basin.

The artist is also an accomplished nature writer with such books as *Outdoors on Foot, Kettle of Hawks, I Was Born in a Tree and Raised by Bees* and the popular sequel, *Crinkleroot's Animal Tracks and Wildlife Signs* to his credit. His resolve to look anew at everything he planned to draw for this book has resulted in artwork of surprising vigor and freshness.

 *Afterword*

All ancient people personified the forces and elements of nature. For the Greeks, the god Zeus represented thunder and lightning, Boreas the north wind, Triton the sea, Demeter was the goddess of useful crops, and a lovely young woman symbolized water emerging from a spring in a meadow or wood. But it is not easy to imagine how a single person could represent water itself. Although water seems chemically simple, with its short formula H_2O, it can take forms as different as the placid surface of a lake on a windless day, the friendly steam emerging from a tea kettle, or the frightening harshness of an iceberg.

The authors of *Raindrop Stories* have chosen a child to symbolize that water can take multiple aspects yet remain fundamentally the same element, H_2O. Like water, the child appears simple under ordinary circumstances, yet is as versatile as this element, unpredictably displaying a wide range of moods in response to different surroundings and events. Almost any ordinary boy or girl could serve to personify the many forms that water takes in nature because Joan as well as Johnny is highly responsive to any change in the world.

Like other good fables, *Raindrop Stories* convey with charm and great clarity a complex and universal truth. It is that all aspects of creation take different forms, and play different roles, depending upon the circumstances under which they develop and function.

René Dubos, author of *So Human an Animal*
The Rockefeller University, New York, N.Y.